Dinosa Monument

by Leigh Clark

Harcourt
SCHOOL PUBLISHERS

p.3, ©Louie Psihoyos/Science Faction/Getty Images; p.4-5, ©Gerald & Buff Corsi/Visuals Unlimited; p.6, ©James L. Amos/CORBIS; p.7, ©Francois Gohier/Photo Researchers, Inc.; p. 8-9, Joe LeMonnier: p.10, ©Scott W. Smith/Animals Animals; p.11, ©Greg Martin/SuperStock; p.12, ©Francois Gohier/Photo Researchers, Inc.; p.14, ©Dave G. Houser/Post-Houserstock/Corbis.

Printed in China

ISBN 10: 0-15-350533-8
ISBN 13: 978-0-15-350533-1

Ordering Options
ISBN 10: 0-15-350334-3 (Grade 4 Below-Level Collection)
ISBN 13: 978-0-15-350533-1 (Grade 4 Below-Level Collection)
ISBN 10: 0-15-357528-X (package of 5)
ISBN 13: 978-0-15-357528-0 (package of 5)

4 5 6 7 8 9 10 0940 12 11 10 09

Somewhere on a mountain in Utah, a worker chips away at a rock. Gradually the pieces of rock fall away, and the bones of a dinosaur appear.

This worker and many others at Dinosaur National Monument in Utah spend their day searching for fossils. A fossil is the remains of an animal that lived long ago. It could be a bone or a footprint that has hardened in stone.

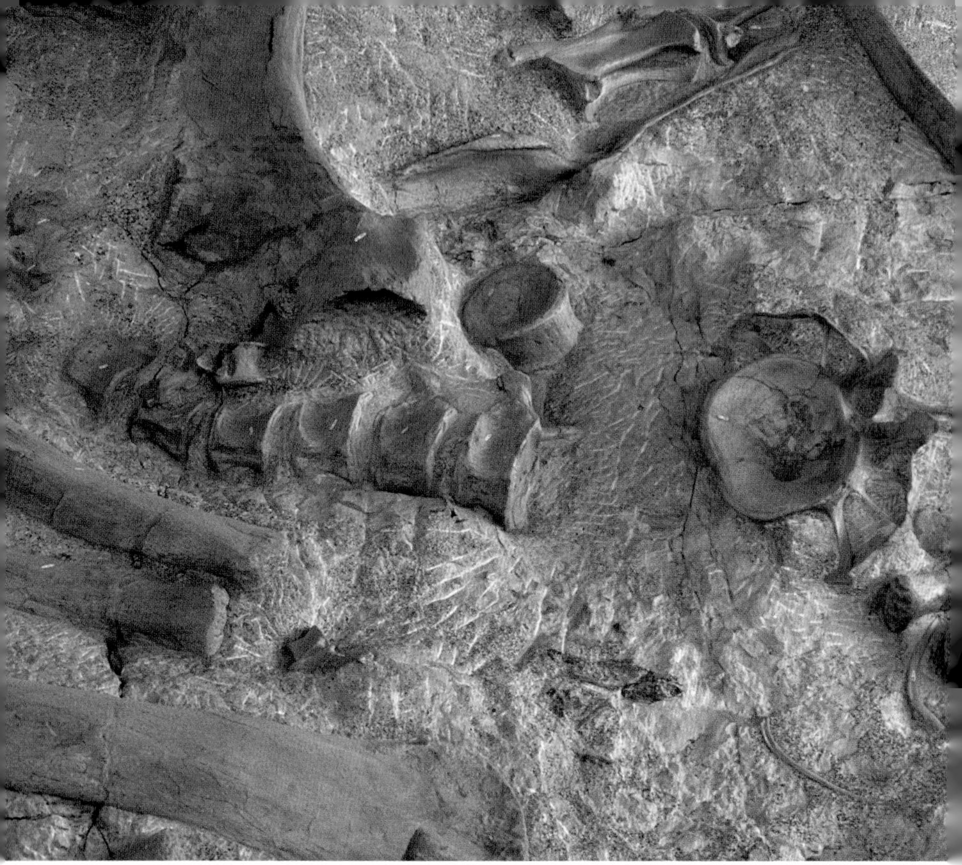

Millions of years ago, dinosaurs lived in much of the land that is now the United States. Over the years, as the dinosaurs died out, many of their bodies sank into the Earth and formed fossils. Fossils are not the real bones of a dinosaur. As years pass, materials in Earth replace the bones. These materials form copies of the bones. These copies are called fossils.

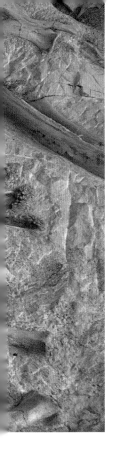

In the early 1900s, a scientist named Earl Douglas began to search for fossil bones. He knew that other fossils had been found in states that were near Utah. Then one day he saw the tailbone of an enormous dinosaur submerged in the rock.

The fossil bones that Douglas found turned out to be those of the Apatosaurus. This was one of the most massive dinosaurs that ever lived. The fossils made up the entire body of the dinosaur. It was one of the most exciting dinosaur finds in history.

Douglas found the fossils in a huge pit that was filled with rock and stone. In the pit, the fossils of thousands of other dinosaurs were discovered. Workers began to dig up the fossils. By the time the digging was finished, fossils of at least nine different kinds of dinosaurs had been found.

For the next fifteen years, workers dug
thousands of fossil bones out of the pit. They
were shipped to a museum where the bones were
tagged and studied.

Putting together the skeletons of dinosaurs is
complicated work. Most skeletons you see are not
the bones of one whole dinosaur. Whole bodies
of dinosaur bones are not often found. The bones
usually come from several animals. Sometimes fake
bones are used to complete a skeleton when the
real bones cannot be found.

When putting together a dinosaur, scientists face many obstacles. They must first determine the type of bone. Then they sort the bones. The shape of the bone tells whether the bone is a leg bone, a hip bone, teeth, claws, or feet. Then the bones are pieced together like a giant puzzle.

The bones give the scientists a good idea of how big the dinosaur may have been in real life. Teeth tell a lot about the dinosaur. Sharp teeth mean a dinosaur ate meat, and flat teeth are found in dinosaurs that ate plants.

How did all those dinosaur bones end up in one place? Millions of years ago, a river flowed through the land where the dinosaurs roamed. Sometimes a dinosaur would die near the river. When the river flooded, the body was washed away. It was carried down the river and became stuck in a sandbar. Eventually the body became buried with sand and mud. Sometimes the bones broke apart. Over millions of years, the bones piled up at the bottom of the river.

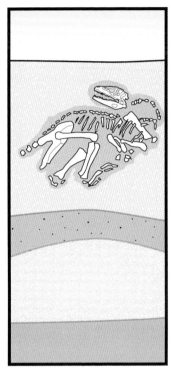
Dinosaur bones

As millions of years passed, the river dried up. The sand and mud that was at the bottom of the river became extremely hard. New sand and rock formed layers over the dinosaur bones.

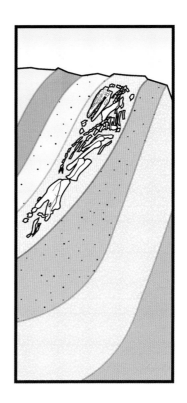

Bones on sandbar   Bones begin to appear

Then mountains began to form. The forces under the Earth pushed the mountains upward. The section of Earth that contained the dinosaur bones was now above the ground. As rain, wind, and frost wore away parts of the mountains, some of the dinosaur bones began to appear. That is when Earl Douglas spotted the Apatosaurus bones.

In 1915, the pit that held the dinosaur bones became Dinosaur National Monument. The creation of the monument protected the dinosaur bones. In 1958, a visitors' center was built so that people could examine the bones. Today this building is called Dinosaur Quarry.

One interesting thing about the Dinosaur Quarry is that the rear wall of the building is actually part of the dinosaur pit! There, you can see over 1,400 bones still in the rock. That must be a very eerie sight!

Visitors can observe workers as they remove bones from the large wall. To do this, workers need a number of tools and contraptions. Jackhammers break up the large pieces of rock. Picks and chisels are used to break apart the smaller rocks. The workers must be extremely careful not to break the dinosaur fossils.

Once the bones are removed, they are taken to the laboratory. There, scientists measure and record the sizes of the fossil bones. Then they compare them with other bones to try to determine what the bones are.

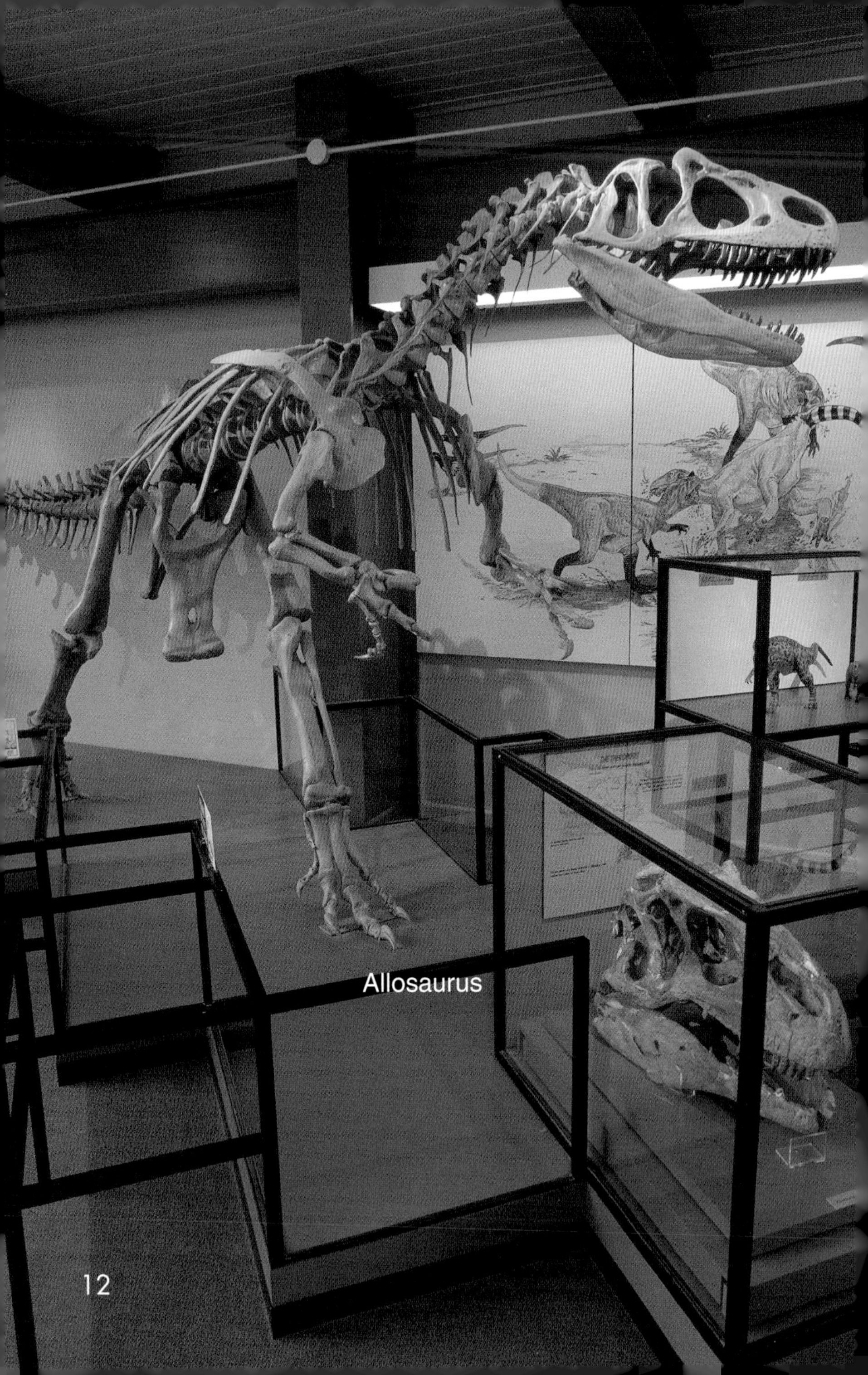

Allosaurus

The bones found at the pit came from many dinosaurs. One was the elegant, long-necked Apatosaurus. This animal is still the largest animal to have ever walked on Earth. The Apatosaurus that Douglas found was over 76 feet (23 m) long! This plant-eating dinosaur walked on all four legs. Its legs had to be very sturdy to hold up its huge body.

Some bird-like dinosaurs found at the pit walked on only two legs. These dinosaurs were also fairly small. One, called Dryosaurus, stood only about 6 feet (1.83 m) tall. That's not very big for a dinosaur! These dinosaurs could run very quickly on two legs! They were plant eaters.

Another dinosaur, the Allosaurus, was a meat-eating animal. It was probably one of the scariest dinosaurs that ever lived. It also walked on two legs. It most likely used its front claws to grab its prey. This dinosaur stood about 30 feet (9.14 m) tall.

   As years pass, people gather more information about dinosaurs. Their fossils tell us about what life was like millions of years ago. Now we know that some dinosaurs may have lived in groups. They were fast-moving animals, and many were very clever hunters.

   We still don't know exactly why dinosaurs are extinct. *Extinct* means that they "died out." Maybe the answer lies somewhere deep inside the Earth. Perhaps one day we will know what happened to these mighty animals that lived so long ago.

Think Critically

1. How did so many dinosaur bones end up at Dinosaur National Monument?

2. What is the first thing a worker must do when trying to put together the skeleton of a dinosaur?

3. Why was Earl Douglas's discovery so important?

4. What have scientists learned about dinosaurs that might have surprised them?

5. Would you like to visit Dinosaur National Monument some day? Explain why or why not.

 Science

Dinosaur Puzzle Find out about a dinosaur that interests you, and make an accurate drawing of it. Then cut up your drawing to create your own dinosaur puzzle.

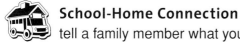 **School-Home Connection** In your own words, tell a family member what you learned about dinosaurs.